CURRIER & IVES
DINNERWARE

Debbie & Randy Coe

Schiffer Publishing Ltd

4880 Lower Valley Road · Atglen, PA 19310

Copyright © 2015 by Debbie and Randy Coe

Library of Congress Control Number: 2015932456

Designed by Brenda McCallum
Cover design by Justin Watkinson
Type set in Colonna MT/Times New Roman

ISBN: 978-0-7643-4949-2
Printed in China

Published by Schiffer Publishing, Ltd.
4880 Lower Valley Road
Atglen, PA 19310
Phone: (610) 593-1777; Fax: (610) 593-2002
E-mail: Info@schifferbooks.com

For our complete selection of fine books on this and related subjects, please visit our website at www.schifferbooks.com. You may also write for a free catalog.

This book may be purchased from the publisher. Please try your bookstore first.

We are always looking for people to write books on new and related subjects. If you have an idea for a book, please contact us at proposals@schifferbooks.com.

Schiffer Publishing's titles are available at special discounts for bulk purchases for sales promotions or premiums. Special editions, including personalized covers, corporate imprints, and excerpts can be created in large quantities for special needs. For more information, contact the publisher.

CONTENTS

Acknowledgments 4

Foreword 5

Currier & Ives: Historical Background 6

Royal China Company 19

    Measurements 21

    Value Guide 21

    Back Stamps 22

Shapes 26

    Ashtray 26

    Bowls 27

    Butter 35

    Candy Dish 37

    Casserole 38

    Clock 41

    Creamers 42

    Cup and Saucer 44

    Deviled Egg Dish 45

    Gravy Boat and Liner 46

    Hostette Table 52

    Hurricane Lamp 53

    Mugs 54

    Pastry Server 55

    Pie Bakers................................. 56

    Plates 63

    Platter 78

    Shakers 79

    Sugar Bowls with Lids 81

    Teapots 85

    Tidbit Server 87

    Tray 88

    Tile Trivet 89

    Wall Plaques 90

Other Currier and Ives Dinnerware 91

Glassware Go-Alongs 92

Collector Information 106

Bibliography 108

Index 110

ACKNOWLEDGMENTS

The following people permitted us to photograph their pieces at shows, in their homes, or at antique malls. Because of their generosity, this book contains a vast assortment of beautiful pieces of dinnerware. We are deeply indebted to Laura Gibbs; Patricia Martin; Shirley Moore; and Roberta Watkins for sharing their collections with us.

The people at Replacements, Ltd., provided us with some awesome assistance. The founder and current CEO, Bob Page, along with his partner, Dale Fredrickson, granted us permission to use the Currier and Ives pieces they had in their inventory. Jaime Robinson, a terrific friend, who is also a researcher at Replacememts, was instrumental in getting the information assembled and sent to us. He also provided us with some background and marketing information about the dinnerware and oven ware items. Lisa Conklin, the Public Relations Manager, was a big help with our licensing agreement. We greatly appreciate having access to these pieces to further enhance this book. It is an enormous compliment to us that all of these individuals took the time to provide us accurate information.

As we were completing book on this book, we found we were still in need of some information. We contacted Tim Merli, the president of the Currier and Ives Collector's Club and he was very helpful in getting the information and photos that we needed. He graciously provided us a lot of additional information along with the photos we were in need of. We greatly appreciate all the assistance he provided to us. Tim was very generous with his knowledge and time. We also had an additional member of the club, who wished to remain anonymous, provide us with some great photos too.

As in all of our projects, this book could not have come together without all the effort of many people. Each and every piece of information, whether it be small or big, contributes to the large picture. When it all comes together, the final result is a presentation of facts and photos in book form that can be enjoyed and used by all of you.

A huge thank you to everyone.

Our interest in doing this book about Currier and Ives dinnerware, the ever popular blue and white dinnerware that gives a historic background to the American way of life, came from many of our customers. They were looking for information about their dinnerware and complained that there was no reference book on the subject.

People have long been attracted to dinnerware that features American historic events and scenes. The Currier and Ives illustrations on this dinnerware portray average people in everyday activities around America during the late nineteenth century. The designs are so realistic that you can almost feel part of what the people were experiencing.

There has been a lack of information about this dinnerware pattern and we are frequently asked a variety of questions about it. This information void has encouraged us to research this topic extensively. It is amazing what we have learned and we are happy to be able to share it with all of our readers. It is our hope that this book will help you appreciate your dinnerware even more.

In a time when most of the new dinnerware being sold in America is made in China, Currier and Ives dinnerware has the big plus that it was made in America and features American scenes.

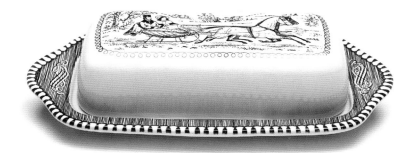

CURRIER & IVES:
Historical Background

To get a grasp on the importance of the art work of Currier and Ives, you have to first step back into American history and understand what was going on when they were active. Andrew Jackson became the seventh American president in 1829. The South was filled with plantations worked by slaves. The Civil War had yet to begin. Agriculture was the main source of livelihood for many people. Our current state of Texas was then part of Mexico. The West was still an unknown wilderness area controlled by Native Americans. Railroads were a new form of transportation.

John and William Pendleton established their Boston printing company in 1824 and were the first to make a success of the new lithographic process. Four years later, their business had grown so much that it needed to hire an additional employee. An apprenticeship was offered to Nathaniel Currier (1813–1888), who was only fifteen years old at the time. He was a very smart young man and quickly learned their new lithographic technique. He obtained the skills needed to excel in this new type of printing.

In 1834, he left the Pendletons to open his own printing company. Currier formed a short lived partnership with a man named Stodart in New York City. After a year, it became obvious the situation wasn't working and the partnership dissolved. Currier set up his own company at 1 Wall Street, naming it "N. Currier, Lithographer." Though mainly a job printer focused on producing a variety of items for his clients, he began to experiment with the production of lithographic prints of various historic events. In 1840, the steamship *Lexington* burned in Long Island Sound, taking over one hundred lives. Currier made a print of the tragedy that quickly sold out to an eager public and gained him a national reputation. With this new success, he was able to expand his business, hiring his brother Charles and teaching him the trade. Charles sporadically worked for his brother over the years, but also had his own lithography business. He was the inventor of a lithographic crayon that he called Crayola.

Charles's most important contribution to the company may have been the introduction of his brother to James Merritt Ives, the husband of his wife's sister. In 1852, the company was growing and needed a bookkeeper. This simple decision would prove to have a huge future impact on the future of Currier Company. Charles suggested that his brother hire Ives. Born in 1824, Ives was a professional bookkeeper, but also had some experience in lithography and was a self-taught artist. He had a love of art and was a frequent visitor to many galleries. He excelled at the new job and, by 1857, became a partner in the firm, which was renamed "Currier & Ives." When the Civil War broke out in 1861, Ives was 37 years old and, while he could have avoided serving, felt the need to join the Union army. He was captain of a regiment from Brooklyn. Once the war ended, Ives came back to work at the printing company.

At their studios at 33 Spruce Street, Currier & Ives created many of the designs for their lithographic prints, but not all of them. They employed or contracted with many notable artists of the day to create images and prepare the lithograph stones. The artists included: James E. Butterworth; John Cameron; George Durrie; Eastman Johnson; Otto Knirsch; Louis Maurer; Fanny Palmer; Charles Parsons; Napoleon Sarony; J. Schultz; C. Severin; Arthur Fitzwilliam Tait; Franz Venino; William Walker; and Thomas Worth.

Once the prints were made, a team of women hand colored them. Following a master print, each woman would only apply one color and then hand off the print to the next to add another color. When all the colors were applied, a "finisher" would look over the print to check for quality and apply any touch paint that may have been needed.

The ideas for the prints came from all aspects of life and featured attitudes, celebrations, customs, habits, social events, and work ethics. In all, they produced over 7500 different titles. The American public dearly loved their creations, buying in excess of one million prints between 1835 and 1907.

Nathaniel Currier retired in 1880 and turned over his control to his son, Edward. Eight years later, Nathaniel died of a heart attack. James Merritt Ives's son, Chauncey took over from his father in 1895. A few months later, the senior Ives passed away. Even with the loss of the original partners, not much changed at the company. In 1902, Edward Currier sold his share to Chauncey Ives. New developments in offset printing and photo engraving encroached on the printer's business, and left the company unable to compete with newspapers, which now carried front page photos of American events. In 1907, Chauncey Ives liquidated the company.

This famous partnership left a deep impression on people of its time that has continues into the present. The work of Nathaniel Currier and James Merritt Ives has become iconic, which is why it is often referred to as the "Image" of America. Their prints captured the heritage of America from 1835 to 1907, and it was not long before the Currier and Ives designs were being adapted for several types of media.

Currier & Ives
Prints Used on China Patterns

The Royal China usually used "excerpts" from the original Currier & Ives prints. For the readers convenience the complete image of most of the lithographs used by Royal China Company are printed below. These images are named with the original title on the lithograph. As you will see, the china pattern titles were often shortened and sometimes punctuated or spelled differently than the original prints.

Currier & Ives lithographs for two images used on the china could not be found: "Old Inn–Winter, and "The Schoolhouse in Winter." Both of these are based on art by George Henry Durrie, who was a Currier & Ives artist. Old Inn, is a loose rendition of an oil painting entitled *On the Road to Boston*, which Durrie painted in 1861. (It most recently sold at Sotheby's in 2013 and can be seen at http://www.sothebys.com/en/auctions/ecatalogue/2013/american-art-n09048/lot.34.html.) "The Schoolhouse" was derived from Durrie's painting, *The Red School House,* now in the Metropolitan Museum of Art, New York. It is not known if Currier & Ives published lithographs of these two images.

Currier & Ives made lithographs of ten of Durrie's works beginning in 1850. These include *Winter in the Country: Old Grist Mill* and *Winter in the Country: Getting Ice,* which are found on china patterns.

For the interested reader, the Library of Congress has a large number of Currier & Ives prints available on line (www.loc.gov).

American Homestead Winter

The Birth-place of Washington, At Bridges Creek, Westmoreland Co.Va (Feby. 22nd 1732)

Central Park, the Drive

Clipper Ship Dreadnought— Off Tuskar Light

Early Winter

9

The
Express Train

Fashionable
"Turn-outs" in
Central Park

Harvest

A Home on the
Mississippi

Home,
Sweet Home

Home to
Thanksgiving

11

*Low Water
in the Mississippi*

*Maple Sugaring:
Early Spring in the
Northern Woods*

*Midnight Race
on the Mississippi*

*The Old
Farm Gate*

*The Old
Oaken Bucket*

*On the
Mississippi:
Loading Cotton*

13

Preparing for Market

The Return from the Pasture

The Road, —Winter

Rocky Mountains.
Emigrants Crossing
the Plains

The
Sleigh Race

A Snowy
Morning

15

*The Star
of the Road*

*A Suburban
Retreat*

*Trolling for
Blue Fish*

*The
Trout Stream*

*Winter in the
Country:
Getting Ice*

*Winter in the
Country: The Old
Grist Mill*

17

Woodcock Shooting

The "Schoolhouse in Winter" pattern is actually from a painting entitle *The Red School House* by George Henry Durrie, though the look is certainly similar to Currier & Ives. The original painting is in the Metropolitan Museum of Art, New York. Currier & Ives made lithographs of ten of Durrie's works beginning in 1850. These include *Winter in the Country: Old Grist Mill* and *Winter in the Country: Getting Ice*, which are found on china patterns. It is not known if Currier & Ives published a lithograph of this image.

A close version of this image, *On the Road to Boston*, by George Henry Durrie, was the basis of the "Old Inn-Winter" pattern. It is not known if Currier & Ives published a lithograph of this image.

Left: starter set in original box, 10.75" square. Right top: dinner plate,
10" wide; right bottom: cup, 2.25" tall; saucer, 6" wide.

ROYAL CHINA COMPANY

The old site of the Sebring China Company in Sebring, Ohio, was a great
location for the new Royal China Company, founded in 1934. The founders of
this company included John Briggs, William Hebenstreit, and Beatrice Miller,
who three had extensive business experience. Both Hebenstreit and Miller
came from the National Publicity Bureau located in Omaha, Nebraska, where
they produced premiums for various companies. Briggs was a local potter.
Together, their expertise offered a winning combination that set the company
on a very productive path.

Their initial products were premiums for the National Publicity Bureau.
Following its success with them, the company moved on to produce over-glaze
decal dinnerware. As time went on, it became obvious that Miller was driving
the direction of the company.

In 1948, Kenneth Doyle, from the printing business, came up with an idea for a machine that would change the way designs were applied to dinnerware. Instead of stamping a design on paper and transferring it to the pottery, the machine stamped the pattern directly onto the raw pottery. As you can imagine, this innovation rapidly changed the way dinnerware was made, making it possible for pattern to be mass-produced at a reduced cost. The use of decals was abandoned in the next two years.

In 1949, the Royal China Company began to create a new style of dinnerware based on the Currier and Ives prints. By this time, the prints were in the public domain, so no special permission was needed to use them on their dinnerware. Currier and Ives themes were used for each of the particular pieces of the attractive dinnerware. Gordon Parker created a special scrolled border to go with the scene. He had served as the Art Director at Royal China.

The dinnerware was made in six colors: Black, Blue, Brown, Gray, Green, and Pink, along with some pieces in multi-colors. Blue was by far the most popular, so it is now, of course, the easiest to find. At its introduction, the pattern was widely popular and sales took off. Through the next twenty years, Currier and Ives dinnerware continued to sell well for the company.

With an eye to future expansion, Royal purchased the French Saxon China Company in 1964; its building was located next door to the Royal factory. In 1969, Royal China was sold to Jeannette Glass Company. The Royal China factory caught fire in February 1970 and was completely destroyed. As luck would have it, the vacant former French Saxon China building next door permitted the company to relocate quickly, so there was no major loss of sales.

As they started over, the executives at Jeannette Glass made a decision to eliminate the Currier & Ives line, along with their Colonial Homestead, Old Curiosity Shop, and Bucks Country lines from the Royal China offerings. The new owners felt that the designs of these patterns were too old and that the public wanted something fresh. With the poor sales that resulted, it soon became obvious that this decision was way off base.

The Jeannette Glass management realized they were wrong and, by popular request, Currier and Ives dinnerware was reintroduced in 1975. While the basic place settings were continued, some new items were introduced in a slightly different style. The Currier and Ives scene remained in the center of the pieces, but the scrolled border was eliminated from the design. Five- and eight-piece hostess sets also were offered. The five-piece set consisted of a cake plate, pie baker, deviled egg plate, candy dish, and dip bowl. The eight-piece set included a cake plate, pie baker, and six dessert plates. Their quality and color were not the same as those that had been produced by Royal China, and the sales never equaled what Royal China had achieved.

The Currier and Ives pattern was continued until the company was sold to Coca Cola in 1976. J Corporation purchased the company in 1981 and operated it, until 1984, even though not much dinnerware was made. Nordic Capitol bought the company and operated it until 1986 when bankruptcy was declared. The time-honored tradition of fine dinnerware was now officially over.

Through the years, Currier and Ives dinnerware could be purchased in many different ways. The most most extensive distribution was through various supermarkets, but primarily through A & P and Winn Dixie. Each week, a different piece was made available for purchase or to be given as a premium based on the amount of groceries bought. The dinnerware was also offered in the S & H Green Stamp catalog, and both Montgomery Ward and Sears carried the dishes in their catalogs and stores. In later years, Kmart also carried the dish line.

MEASUREMENTS

There is some variations in size from one piece to the next. Catalog listings will show a size from the mould. As the pottery worker handles each piece, the size can change. Green ware can be one size, but as it is fired and cools, there is some variation. Actual height and width measurements were taken off each piece of dinnerware as it was photographed.

VALUE GUIDE

All the values shown in this book are for dinnerware in **Mint Condition only**. Any type of damage will diminish the value of the piece. The discounted value should reflect the extent of the damage and whether it hurts the appearance of the piece. An air bubble in the glaze would be considered minimal compared to a huge crack. Any stains will also decrease the value. The blue color can vary from a nice dark blue to a lighter blue. Pieces that have been repaired also should carry a value that is far below normal, depending on their appearance.

Collectors and dealers both were consulted to contribute values so we could obtain a true reflection of the current market. The listed values have been derived from actual dealer sales, what collectors have paid, prices seen at shows, auction results, and national publications. As with any type of collectible, there are some regional differences in supply and demand.

Ultimately, the collector needs to decide what they would be willing pay for a specific item. The authors have tried to list **sustainable values** and not those for isolated pieces that may have sold for record amounts. The job of our consultants was to report the prices that were found, not to set values based on their opinions. This book is to be used only as a guide when determining what an item is worth; our estimates are based on available information. While some items will appreciate in value, others will go down based on the supply and demand for the piece. This reality is not popular, but is one that has become accepted by most dealers and collectors.

Neither the author nor the publisher assumes any responsibility for transactions that may occur based of this book.

BACK STAMPS

Royal China marked many of their items, but not all of them. Each mark was hand-applied to the item, followed by a crystal glaze applied over the entire piece and then fired on, giving it a permanent gloss finish. Here is a selection of the different back stamps we have run across. During various times, there were different marks put on the pieces. On some of the items, the mark includes the name of the scene that was used.

Detail of back stamp with "Fashionable Turnouts"

Detail of back stamp with "Early Winter"

Detail of back stamp with "The Old Grist Mill"

Detail of back stamp with "The Rocky Mountains"

Detail of back stamp with "Maple Sugaring"

Detail of back stamp of Royal China, Sebring, Ohio, with a crown

Detail of back stamp of Royal China / Sebring, Ohio / Americana / Currier and Ives

Detail of back stamp of Royal China on / Royal-Ironstone

Detail of back stamp of Royal China / Jeannette Corporation / Currier and Ives

SHAPES

Being a dinnerware pattern, all kinds of shapes were manufactured that could be used nicely to set a table for any meal. Several wonderful accessory items were also made, along with some items meant to decorate your kitchen or dining room areas. The shapes are arranged in alphabetical order for convenience in locating them.

ASHTRAY

The **ashtray** depicts a scene from Central Park in New York City called *Central Park, The Drive*. Central Park was a center of bustling activity during this time period. Family and friends frequently got together for various activities. In the lithograph, a couple is sitting on bench watching what is going on. Along the road are riders on horses and buggies being pulled along by a team of horses. Along the path are families and friends stopping to visit

There are three white indents for holding cigarettes. There has been no back stamp found on this piece.

Ashtray, *Central Park, the Drive* scene, 5.5" wide; no back stamp.
$12.00

Fruit Bowl

The **fruit bowl** shows the scene called *The Old Farm Gate*. Children are playing on the gate, which is an entrance to the family farm. In front of the gate is the family dog, jumping in excitement at what the kids are doing.

Fruit bowl, *The Old Farm Gate* scene, 5.6" wide; no back stamp.
$6.50. **Note:** shown upright

Fruit bowl, shown flat

Detail of *The Old Farm Gate* scene

Cereal Bowls

There are two versions of the **cereal bowl**, each having a different scene on it. The first bowl is round and has no handles. It features the scene called "The Schoolhouse in Winter." The snow on the ground and the school house makes its obvious that winter has arrived. The children are playing outside, waiting for school to start. Along the road is a man in a sled being pulled by horses, going by the school. The bowl has been found with and without a back stamp.

The other style has small handles and is rather hard to find. At the time this bowl was introduced the handles were referred into lug handles. Today most collectors just call them tab handles. *A Suburban Retreat* is the scene on this bowl. In the background is a beautiful two-story house. Boats are shown sailing across a lake. In the front is a mother sitting on a bench with her two daughters. The bowl has been found with and without back stamps.

Cereal bowl, "The Schoolhouse in Winter" scene, 6.75" wide; no back stamp, USA mark. **$12.50**. **Note:** Shown upright

Cereal bowl, shown flat

Cereal bowl, *A Suburban Retreat scene*, with tab handles, 7.15" wide;
back stamp. **$29.50**

Dip Bowl

The **dip bowl** is plain white and easily missed. The shape is the same as the foot of the pedestal cake plate (see page 75). There is no mark on it. The bowl was listed in the 1984 price list, but there is a mystery about it. This piece had no specific other item with which it was used, though it could be used on the snack plate with the indent instead of the mug. Why does it exist? Our guess is that an accompanying piece was planned, but the production never occurred.

Note: This piece is not shown separately but can be viewed with the pedestal cake plate.

Rim Soup Bowl

The **rim soup bowl** has the *Early Winter* scene. A group of ice skaters is on the local pond. To the left is a two-story house covered in snow. There are wheel tracks in the snow on the road. There is a back stamp on the bowl.

Rim soup bowl, *Early Winter* scene, 8.5" wide; marked on bottom. **$12.50**

Detail of *Early Winter* scene

Rim soup bowl, *Early Winter* scene, pink version, 8.5" wide; marked on bottom "Currier & Ives by Royal China Royal—Ironstone Made in USA Detergent Proof Oven Proof Dish Washer Safe Underglaze." **$9.50**. **Note:** Several of the items were made in pink, but most collectors just want the blue.

Vegetable Bowl

The **vegetable bowl** has two versions, with two different scenes. The first bowl is shallow and has the *Maple Sugaring* scene. When the cold weather sets in, the sap on the maple trees is ready to be tapped. This is a popular activity in the northeastern states. The sap from the maple tree is extracted into buckets hanging on the trees. It is gathered and poured into a large kettle, where it is boiled and processed to make syrup. The men are watching over the pots of sap as they boil down the liquid to make syrup. This activity provided an income for many families in the area. This bowl does have a back stamp.

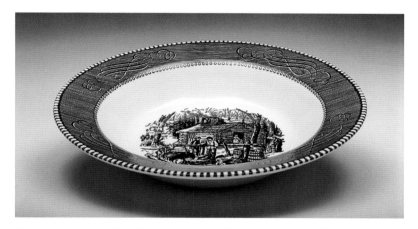

Vegetable bowl, shallow, *Maple Sugaring: Early Spring in the Northern Woods* scene, 9" wide; marked on bottom. **$19.50**

Detail of *Maple Sugaring* scene

The other vegetable bowl is deep and has the *Home, Sweet Home* scene on it. Apparently the father is heading home after a long day at work. His children are at the gate to greet him. The family dog is bouncing in excitement to see "Dad."

Vegetable bowl, deep, *Home, Sweet Home* scene, 10" wide; no back stamp. **$34.50**

BUTTER DISH, COVERED, QUARTER-POUND STYLE

The two-piece **covered butter dish** comes in two versions with similar scenes. The most commonly found version is called *The Road, —Winter*, and the other is called *Fashionable "Turn-outs" in Central Park*. Both versions will have the same scene on the top of the lid and on the top of the bottom piece. *The Road, —Winter* features a couple dressed warmly and seated in a horse-drawn sleigh. One horse is a dappled gray and the other is a chestnut color. *Fashionable "Turn-outs" in Central Park* features elegantly dressed couples sitting in fancy carriage. It is being pulled by a horse that is racing along with other horses. It would appear that the couples are showing off what they are wearing, possibly their Sunday best!

Covered butter, quarter-pound, *The Road, –Winter* scene, 7.75" long, 3.8" wide; no mark on bottom. **$29.50**

Covered butter, *The Road, –Winter* scene, shown apart

Covered butter, quarter-pound, *Fashionable "Turn-outs" in Central Park* scene, 7.75" long, 3.8" wide; no mark on bottom. **$36.50**

CANDY DISH, OPEN

This **open candy dish** was from the Hostess Line. It is completely white except for the blue scene in the center that features the *Maple Sugaring* scene. This is the same scene that is found on the shallow vegetable bowl. Like all of the Hostess items, this piece has the rope-style edge.

Candy dish, *Maple Sugaring* scene, rope edge, 8" wide, Hostess Line. **$250.00**

CASSEROLES, COVERED

There are three versions of the **covered casserole**, all with the same scene, *Fashionable Turn-outs in Central Park*, on the side. This scene is also found on the butter.

Covered casserole with open handles, 3.25" tall, 10.5" wide (not including handles); no mark on the bottom. **$65.00**. Lid has scene of *Central Park, the Drive*; bottom has scene of *Fashionable "Turn-outs" in Central Park*. **Note:** shown together

Covered casserole with open handles, shown apart

Covered casserole with open handles, shown apart

Detail on bottom of covered casserole with open handles, *Fashionable "Turn-outs" in Central Park* scene

Detail on knob of covered casserole with open handles, *Central Park, the Drive*

39

One version has open handles on the side and is the most commonly found. *Central Park, the Drive* is on the lid (the ashtray also features this scene). The second version has white tab handles and a plain white lid. The third version also has white tab handles and has the *Central Park, the Drive* scene on the lid. Both of the tab-handled versions command a higher price, since there seem to be fewer of these styles found.

Covered casserole with white tab handles, 3.25" tall, 10.5" wide (not including handles); no mark on the bottom. Lid is plain white; bottom has scene of *Fashionable "Turn-outs" in Central Park*. **$125.00**

Covered casserole with white tab handles, 3.25" tall, 10.5" wide (not including handles); no mark on the bottom. Lid has scene of *Central Park, the Drive*, bottom has scene of *Fashionable "Turn-outs" in Central Park*. **$125.00**

CLOCK

A former Royal China employee has stated that there were some **clocks** made as a special order for the Imperial Clock Company. For years, though, the clocks that were found looked as though a home hobbyist had created them. This authentic clock utilizes the 10" dinner plate, but with the scene of "The Schoolhouse in Winter." This same scene is found on the cereal bowl. The clock has the normal scrolled border with a white center and with a small blue scene surrounding the clock movement. The numbers were applied in blue under the glaze. Above the number 6 is the name of Charles Denning.

Clock, "A Schoolhouse in Winter" scene, 10" wide. **$1000.00**

CREAMERS

The **creamers** have two versions, one that is short and the other is a taller, straight-sided version. On the short version, the white handle can be found plain or with the blue scroll pattern on it. Both creamers have *The Express Train* scene on them. This scene shows a steaming locomotive racing down the railroad tracks. People are seated in the passenger cars. No back stamp has been on them.

Creamer, *The Express Train* scene, plain white handle, 3" tall; no mark on the bottom, but there is an embossed capital A on the bottom. **$8.50**

Detail of *The Express Train*

Creamer, *The Express Train* scene, plain white handle, 3.65" tall;
mark on the bottom with an embossed USA. **$35.00**

CUP AND SAUCER

Two different shapes of **cups** have been found. One is shorter with a pointed handle. The other is a little deeper with a rounded handle. Both cups have *The Star of the Road* scene on them, showing a lady seated in a buggy drawn by a pair of dappled horses. The handles can be plain white or have the blue scroll pattern on it. No back stamp has been found on them.

Cup, *Star of the Road* scene, 2" tall. Saucer, *Low Water in the Mississippi* scene, 6.1" wide; no mark on bottom. **$4.50**

Cup, *Star of the Road* scene, 2.5" tall and 3.65" wide; USA on bottom. **$5.00**.
Note: This style of cup with rounded handle is harder to find.

The **saucer** has a scene from the *Low Water in the Mississippi* scene on it. In the original, outside a small house, there is an African-American family. The kids are dancing around. Two paddle boats are seen chugging down the Mississippi River. To the right of one of the boats, there is a small raft. This river scene reminds one of the story of Huck Finn.

Four slightly different saucer shapes have been found. The variations lie in the size of the indented center and the amount of flare on the edge. Since there is not much value in a single saucer, no one seems to care much about having all the saucer shapes.

DEVILED EGG PLATE

The **deviled egg plate** is 11" wide. This was part of the five-piece Hostess Set. It is completely white except for the blue scene in the center that features *Winter in the Country: The Old Grist Mill*. The hurricane lamp has this same scene. This deviled egg plate has proved to be hard to find. Part of this stems from the fact that there are collectors of just deviled egg plates, so these end up in a completely different type of collection.

Deviled egg plate, *Winter in the Country: The Old Grist Mill* scene, 10" wide. **$175.00**

GRAVY BOAT, LINER, AND LADLE

The **gravy boat** features *The Road, –Winter* scene, which is also is the scene on the cover of one version of the butter dish. There are three different gravy boat shapes. One, the easiest to find, has spouted edges. This gravy boat is found in two different versions: one with scrolls below the spout and one without. Those with the scrolls have a smaller scene, while those with no scroll have the space for a larger scene on them.

Gravy boat and liner; no mark on bottom. Gravy boat, *The Road, –Winter* scene, 2.75" tall, 5.75" long; liner, *The Old Oaken Bucket* scene, 8" long. **$29.50**. **Note:** shown together.

Gravy boat and liner

Gravy boat detail

Detail of *The Old Oaken Bucket* scene on gravy liner

Gravy boat variations. Left: small picture with scrolls, **$20**;
Right: large picture without scrolls, **$75**

The second gravy boat shape has white tab handles, and the third version has a small round deep bowl that is reminiscent of a sugar bowl, but there is no indent for a lid. It is 2.75" tall and 6" wide. There has been no back stamp found on these pieces.

Gravy boat, *The Road, –Winter*, with white tab handles,
4.5" wide, 2.75" tall. **$50.00**

The third gravy boat shape is very rare. It is again decorated with *The Road, –Winter* scene, but has no handle or spout.

Gravy boat, **The Road, –Winter** scene, round with no handles, 6" wide, 2.75" tall. **Too rare to price**

There are two different **liners** that match the corresponding gravy boats. The liner for the spouted gravy has small, flared out tab handles. *The Old Oaken Bucket* scene is on this liner, featuring a boy at the well drawing a bucket filled with water to take back to his home (below and page 46).

Gravy boat liner, *The Old Oaken Bucket* scene, flared out tab handles, 8" long.

There are wider plain white tab handles on the other liner which fits the other two gravy boats. It features the *The Birth-place of Washington*, with the small house, overlooking a river, where George Washington was born. A boat is sailing down the river and there is a tree in the yard that has been cut down.

Gravy boat liner, *The Birth-place of Washington* scene, white tab handles, 8" long. **$29.50**

There are three versions of the gravy **ladle**. They are all plain white with no mark on them. The first version has a handle that curves slightly and has a channel on the backside. At the top is a round hole that is about 0.25" wide. The second style is the same shape ,but it is shorter and has no hole at the top. There are two tab feet on the underside of the bowl.

The third version is like the second version, but it has no tab feet. Being all white, the same ladle can be used for other Royal China patterns.

Gravy ladle, white, 0.5" wide hole at end of handle, 7" long, 2.5" wide; no mark, **$30.00**

Gravy ladles, three different styles.
Left: regular style, **$30.00**;
Center: short style with two tab feet, **$40.00**;
Right: short style with no tab feet, **$50.00**

HOSTETTE TABLE OR SWEET SERVER

The **hostette table** or **sweet server** is a free-standing serving item. It is made up of a dinner plate and a chop plate mounted together on wood dowels and set on a three-legged wood base. This nice accessory could be filled with snacks and placed somewhere in the room during a party. In this time period, maple would have been the wood of choice. It is reminiscent of a 1950s smoking stand.

Hostette table, or sweet server, utilizes *The Old Grist Mill* dinner plate and the *A Snowy Morning* chop plate on a wooden stand, 30" tall. **$145.00**

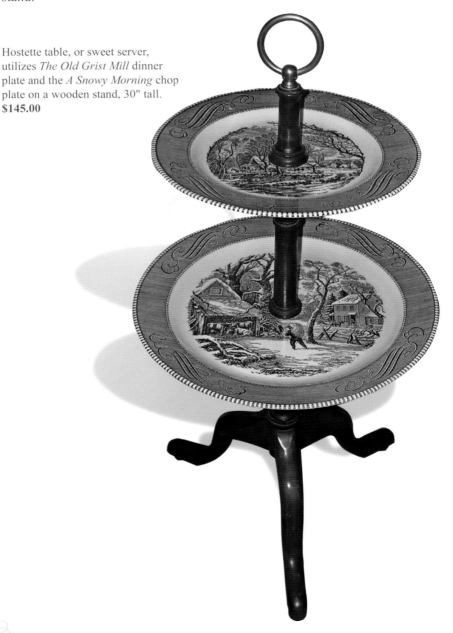

HURRICANE LAMP WITH
GLASS CHIMNEY

The **hurricane lamp** is also referred to as a candle lamp. The base is found with *Winter in the Country: The Old Grist Mill* scene, featuring a man sitting in a wagon filled with bags of grain. In the time period portrayed, grain had to be taken to the grinding mill to make it into flour. To the right of the house is a pair of cows with two people by them. No back stamp has been found on the hurricane base.

The **glass chimney** was made for Royal China under a special order contract. Royal China would seek bids from glass companies to make the chimney for this lamp, according to certain size specifications. To ensure the best price available, the job was annually put out to bid to multiple companies. While it is not known for sure who made the chimneys for Royal China, our best guess is that it was a company from West Virginia. In Salem, West Virginia, alone, there were four companies making lamp chimneys during the 1950s and 1960s: McBride Glass Company, Glass Products Company, Salem Glass Company, and Minners Glass. This hurricane lamp is extremely hard to find complete with the correct chimney. There were three different shapes used. Many times dealers will put a kerosene lamp chimney on the lamp as a replacement, but they don't look right.

Hurricane (candle) lamp, two-piece; base has *The Old Grist Mill* scene; crystal chimney. **$150.00**

Detail of hurricane lamp base.

MUGS

Cocoa

The straight-sided **cocoa mug** has a rounded style of handle, and has *The Express Train* scene on it. This scene is also found on the creamer. While the mug does not have a back stamp on it, the bottom does have the incised USA.

Hot chocolate mug, *The Express Train* scene, 3.25" tall, 10 ounces; USA mark on bottom. **$24.50**

Coffee

The straight-sided **coffee mug** is shorter than the cocoa and has a rounded square handle. *Fashionable "Turn-Outs" in Central Park* is the scene on this mug, which is also found on the casserole. Either a back stamp or the incised USA may be seen on the coffee mug. This mug is hard to find.

Coffee mug, *Fashionable "Turn-outs" in Central Park* scene, 2.75" tall, 8 ounces. **$18.50**

Detail of *Fashionable "Turn-outs" in Central Park* scene

PASTRY SERVER

The **pastry server** (lifter) is from the Hostess Line and is all-white with no markings on it. This makes a nice accessory item for serving cake or pie.

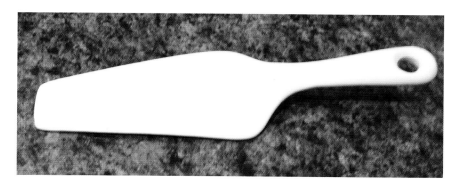

Pastry server, all white, 8" long; Hostess Line; no mark. **$50.00**

PIE BAKERS

Style One

There have been nine different scenes reported to be found on the **pie bakers**. These include: *American Homestead in Winter; Early Winter; Winter in the Country: Getting Ice; A Home on the Mississippi; Maple Sugaring: Early Spring in the Northern Woods; Winter in the Country: The Old Grist Mill;* "*Old Inn—Winter;*" *The Return from the Pasture;* and *A Snowy Morning.* There are variations of a narrow border, a large picture, and small picture. The bakers can be found with and without back stamps. Several of these scenes can also be found on other pieces.

Pie baker, style one, *A Home on the Mississippi* scene, 10" wide, 1.5" tall; marked on bottom with "Royal China Conventional and Microwave Oven Approved Dishwasher Safe USA." **$24.50**

Pie baker, style one, *The Old Grist Mill* scene, 10" wide, 1.5" tall; only marked with "USA" on bottom. **$24.50**

Pie baker, shown flat to show shape

Pie baker, style one, *Early Winter* scene, 10" wide, 1.5" tall;
not marked on bottom. **$24.50. Note:** shown flat and upright

Pie baker, style one, *A Snowy Morning* scene, 10" wide, 1.5" tall; not marked on bottom. **$24.50**

Detail of *A Snowy Morning* scene on the pie baker

Pie baker, *Return from the Pasture* scene; 10" wide, 1.5" tall.
$24.50. **Note:** shown upright and flat

Pie baker,
*A Home on the
Mississippi* scene;
10" wide, 1.5" tall.
$24.50. **Note:**
shown upright
and flat

Pie baker,
Getting Ice scene;
10" wide,
1.5" tall; Hostess
Line. **$24.50**

Style Two

The second style of **pie baker** came from the Hostess line. The baker is white, and some came with a border in a rope-like pattern. In the center was a blue scene featuring *Winter in the Country: Getting Ice*.

Pie baker, style two, *The Road, –Winter* scene; 10" wide, 1.25" tall; marked on back with The Road information; Hostess Line. **$24.50**

Pie baker by Jeanette Corporation, unknown scene with house to left, barn in center, cows under shed, split rail fence in front, two lines going around outside edge, brown color; 10" wide, 1.25" tall; no mark on back. **$24.50**

Pie baker, *The Road, –Winter* scene; 10" wide, 1.5" tall; Hostess Line.
$24.50. **Note:** shown upright and flat

PLATES

Dessert/Bread-and-Butter Plate

The **dessert plate** has also been referred to as the **bread-and-butter plate.** The *Harvest* scene is featured on this plate. After the wheat is cut, the farmer is tying it up the sheaths into bundles to dry. A lady with her child is visiting the men in the field. This plate can be found with and without a back stamp.

Dessert plate, **Harvest** scene; 6"; not marked on the bottom. **$2.50**

Detail of *Harvest* scene

Salad Plate

The **salad plate** features the *The Birth-place of Washington*. No back stamp has been found on this plate. This salad plate is a little harder to find.

Salad plate, *Birth-place of Washington* scene; 7.25" wide; no back stamp. Hard to find, **$8.50**

Snack Plate

The **snack plate** features an offset indented circle for holding the coffee cup. This plate is the same size as the lunch plate. It features the *Winter in the Country: Old Grist Mill* scene.

Snack plate with indented space on side,
The Old Grist Mill scene, 9" wide. **$124.50**

Lunch Plate

Winter in the Country: Old Grist Mill is pictured on the **lunch plate**. It can be found with a back stamp. This plate is difficult to find.

Lunch plate, same as dinner plate, *The Old Grist Mill* scene; 9" wide; has a back stamp. **$18.50**

Dinner Plate

The **dinner plate** is most commonly decorated with *Winter in the Country: Old Grist Mill*. The same scene is also found on the lunch plate. The dinner plate has also been found with multi-colors on it. A version of the dinner plate has been found, decorated with the *Early Winter* scene. It is quite rare, and, at the 2014 convention, it was reported that there had been a purchase price of over $600 for this version.

Dinner plate, *The Old Grist Mill* scene;
10" wide; has a back stamp. **$9.50**

Detail of
*The Old
Grist Mill*

Plates
placed together
to show
difference
in size.
Left: dinner;
Right: lunch

Dinner plate,
pink, *The Old
Grist Mill*
scene; 9.75"
wide. **$14.50**

Dinner plate,
multi-color, *The Old
Grist Mill* scene;
9.75" wide. **$49.50**

Dinner plate, rare
Early Winter scene;
9.75" wide. **$600.00+**

Calendar Plates

Calendar plates were made with a specific year in the center and the different months around the outer edge. The years of 1969 and 1970 were only made in green, while the years 1973 to 1986 were made in blue.

Calendar plate, 1980, 12 calendar pages with 1980 in center, 10" wide;; not marked on the back. **$12.50**

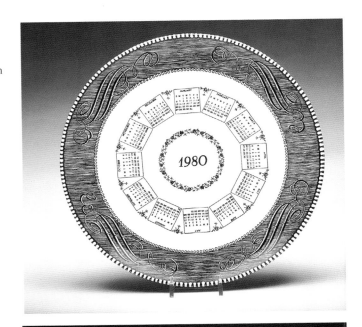

Calendar plate, 1981, 12 calendar pages with 1981 in center, 10" wide; not marked on the back. **$12.50**

Cake Plate

The **cake plate** is from the eight-piece Hostess Set that also had six dessert plates and a pie baker. The *Winter in the Country: Getting Ice* scene is on the cake plate and *American Homestead: Winter* is featured on the dessert plates. The cake plate was meant to hold your favorite cake or pie for serving. The design varied from the regular dinnerware line. The pattern in the center was surrounded by a white border and a rope-like edge. On one of the cake plates, there is listed a recipe for "Miss Mary's Red Velvet Cake."

Left: cake plate, *Getting Ice* scene, rope edge, 10.5" wide; Hostess Line. **$19.50**.
Right: dessert plate, *American Homestead Winter* scene, rope edge, 7.6" wide; Hostess Line. **$9.50**

Detail of Getting Ice scene

Detail of *American Homestead Winter*

Cake plate, *Preparing for Market* scene, rope edge, 10.5" wide; Hostess Line. **$19.50**

Cake plate, *The Sleigh Race* scene, pie crimp edge, 10.5" wide; Hostess Line. **$19.50**

Cake plate, recipe of "Miss Mary's Red Velvet Cake," rope edge, 11.5" wide; Hostess Line; marked on lower left side with "1983 Royal China Co.," no mark on back. **$29.50**

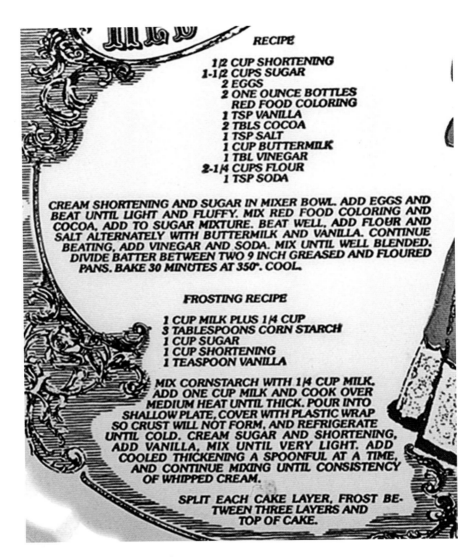

RECIPE

1/2 CUP SHORTENING
1-1/2 CUPS SUGAR
2 EGGS
2 ONE OUNCE BOTTLES
RED FOOD COLORING
1 TSP VANILLA
2 TBLS COCOA
1 TSP SALT
1 CUP BUTTERMILK
1 TBL VINEGAR
2-1/4 CUPS FLOUR
1 TSP SODA

CREAM SHORTENING AND SUGAR IN MIXER BOWL. ADD EGGS AND BEAT UNTIL LIGHT AND FLUFFY. MIX RED FOOD COLORING AND COCOA. ADD TO SUGAR MIXTURE. BEAT WELL, ADD FLOUR AND SALT ALTERNATELY WITH BUTTERMILK AND VANILLA. CONTINUE BEATING, ADD VINEGAR AND SODA. MIX UNTIL WELL BLENDED. DIVIDE BATTER BETWEEN TWO 9 INCH GREASED AND FLOURED PANS. BAKE 30 MINUTES AT 350°. COOL.

FROSTING RECIPE

1 CUP MILK PLUS 1/4 CUP
3 TABLESPOONS CORN STARCH
1 CUP SUGAR
1 CUP SHORTENING
1 TEASPOON VANILLA

MIX CORNSTARCH WITH 1/4 CUP MILK. ADD ONE CUP MILK AND COOK OVER MEDIUM HEAT UNTIL THICK. POUR INTO SHALLOW PLATE, COVER WITH PLASTIC WRAP SO CRUST WILL NOT FORM, AND REFRIGERATE UNTIL COLD. CREAM SUGAR AND SHORTENING, ADD VANILLA, MIX UNTIL VERY LIGHT. ADD COOLED THICKENING A SPOONFUL AT A TIME, AND CONTINUE MIXING UNTIL CONSISTENCY OF WHIPPED CREAM.

SPLIT EACH CAKE LAYER, FROST BE-TWEEN THREE LAYERS AND TOP OF CAKE.

Detail of recipe of Miss Mary's
Velvet Cake on cake plate

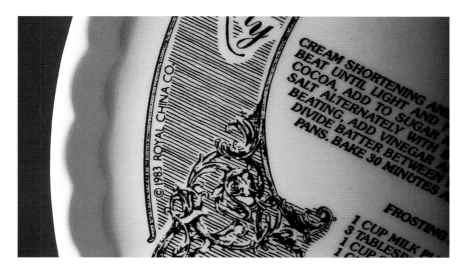

Detail of "1983 Royal China Co." mark

Cake Plate, Pedestal (Footed)

The 10" wide **cake plate** is also found with a pedestal base on the center bottom. The blue pattern in the center is surrounded by a white border and a rope-like edge. On the cake plate is the *Winter in the Country: Getting Ice* scene. The men are out on the lake cutting blocks of ice to use in their kitchens. The blocks, loaded onto the wagon, are taken to the ice house for storage. The bottom side of this piece is all white. The foot resembles a small bowl that has been attached to the plate. This cake plate was offered as part of an eight-piece Hostess Set. Included in this set were six dessert plates and a pie baker.

Pedestal cake plate, *Winter in the Country: Getting Ice* scene, 10.5" wide, 2.75" tall, Hostess Line. **$98.50**.

Chop Plates

There are three sizes of **chop plates**. The 11" chop plate can be found with either the scenes of *Winter in the Country: Getting Ice* or *Rocky Mountains. Emigrants Crossing the Plains.* It usually has a back stamp on it. This plate is hard to find. The 12" plate is only found decorated with "Getting Ice." This one is rarely found with a back stamp. The 13" version features the scene of "A Snowy Morning." Sometimes a back stamp can be found on this plate.

Chop plate, *Rocky Mountains* scene, 11" wide. **$175**. **Note:** this particular scene is hard to find

Chop plate, *Getting Ice* scene, 12" wide; no back stamp. **$12.50**

Detail of *Getting Ice* scene on chop plate

Chop plate, *A Snowy Morning* scene, 13" wide; no back stamp. **$24.50**.

PLATTER, OVAL

The **oval platter** is found with the "Old Inn—Winter" scene, in which a stately two story building is covered with snow. It looks like a cozy place to spend the night away from home. There is no back stamp on this piece.

Platter, oval, "Old Inn—Winter" scene, 13" long, 10" wide; no mark on the back. **$45.00**

Detail of "Old Inn—Winter" scene on platter

SHAKERS, SALT AND PEPPER

On the top of the **salt shaker** is a capital S and on the side is a two-person carriage. A capital P is on the top of the **pepper shaker**. Along the side is the same carriage. The scene is part of the *Fashionable "Turn-outs" in Central Park* lithograph. There is no mark on the shakers.

Shakers, *Fashionable "Turn-outs" in Central Park* scene, plain white handles, 1.7" tall; no back stamp. **$18.50**

Top view of shakers

Detail of *Fashionable "Turn-outs" in Central Park* scene on a shaker

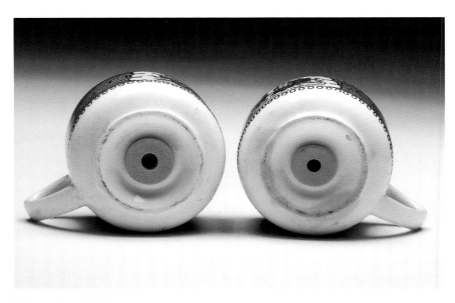

Bottom view of shakers

SUGAR BOWLS WITH LIDS

The sugar bowl is decorated with the *On the Mississippi: Loading Cotton* scene, featuring a stern-wheeler steaming down the river. There are three versions of the sugar bowl. On the first, early version, there is a patterned lid with a large finial. In the 1970s, the lid was changed to be all white, but the large finial was retained. On the third version, the handles were eliminated and the finial on the lid was reduced to a small knob. The only mark is "Made in USA" on the underside of the lid.

Covered sugar, *On the Mississippi: Loading Cotton* scene, plain white handle, scenic lid and knob, 3" tall; no back stamp. **$14.50**

Detail of *On the Mississippi: Loading Cotton* scene

Detail of sugar lid

Covered sugar, *On the Mississippi: Loading Cotton* scene, plain white
handle, scenic lid, white knob, 3" tall; no back stamp. **$14.50**

Covered sugar, *On the Mississippi: Loading Cotton* scene, plain white lid
and white handle, 3" tall, 4" wide; no back stamp. **$75.00**

Covered sugar, *On the Mississippi: Loading Cotton scene*, plain white lid,
no handles, 4" tall; mark on bottom: incised USA. **$50.00**

Covered sugar, *On the Mississippi: Loading Cotton* scene, scenic lid,
no handles, 4" tall; mark on bottom: incised "USA." **$45.00**

Comparison of different sugar lids

TEAPOTS

The **teapot** features the *Clipper Ship Dreadnought–Off Tuskar Light* scene, with sailing ship in full sail in what appears to be stormy, ocean waters. There is a full moon peeking through the clouds. There are two styles of teapot along with two variations. The lids can be patterned all over or only on the top of the finial with the rest being white. The white handle can be plain or have scroll work along the top. There is no back stamp on the teapot.

In the early 1950s, the teapot was first made with a shorter drooped spout. We assume this was done for the ease of pouring the tea. Later, the spout was changed to be slightly longer and straighter. We can only assume that there were been production issues and the change was made because of them.

Teapot, *Clipper Ship Dreadnought–Off Tuskar Light* scene, regular spout, 4" tall, 10.5" long; no back stamp. **$75.00**

Teapot, shown apart

85

Detail of *Clipper Ship Dreadnought–Off Tuskar Light* scene on teapot

Teapot, *Clipper Ship Dreadnought–Off Tuskar Light* scene,
droop spout, 4" tall, 10.5" long; no back stamp. **$150.00**

TIDBIT SERVERS

Three sizes of **tidbit servers** were made—one-tier, two-tier, and three-tier. Different combinations can be found using a fruit bowl, various sizes of plates, and the chop plate. The handle is made of a gold-colored metal.

The hardware was made for Royal China under a special order contract. As with the hurricane lamp chimneys, Royal China put the order, with certain size specifications, out for bid to various metal companies on an annual basis to ensure the best possible price.

Three-tier server. **Top:** fruit bowl with *The Old Farm Gate* scene; **Center:** plate with *Harvest* scene; 6" wide; **Bottom:** lunch plate, *Winter in the Country: The Old Grist Mill* scene, 9" wide. **$85.00**

Three-tier server, shown apart

TILE TRIVET

The **tile trivet** is 6" square and has the *A Snowy Morning* scene, featuring a man hauling hay to feed his cattle that are in the barn on a winter morning. To make the piece more interesting, it can be found two ways: with or without a metal frame. The piece is quite striking with the black metal as an accent. It can be used on the table to hold hot food or, with the metal frame, as a nice decorative item for a kitchen wall.

Tile trivet, *A Snowy Morning* scene, 6" square. **$95.00**

TRAY

This **tray** has tab handles with the pattern flowing out onto them and is decorated with the *Rocky Mountains. Emigrants Crossing the Plains* scene. With the famous, majestic mountains as the back drop, the foreground shows emigrants crossing the plains in a group of covered wagons. This tray is usually found with a back stamp.

Tray, *Rocky Mountains. Emigrants Crossing the Plains* scene, tab handles, 11.5" wide. **$19.50**

Detail of *Rocky Mountains. Emigrants Crossing the Plains* scene

WALL PLAQUES

The **wall plaque** features a partial scene from the *Rocky Mountains. Emigrants Crossing the Plains* picture. There is a group of covered wagons on the trail, being pulled by oxen. On the back are two molded-in holes so the plaque could be hung on the wall. It is marked in capital letters with "CURRIER AND IVES BY ROYAL." This piece also can be found without the molded holes on the back. It can be used as a spoon rest.

This piece can be found in both all blue and multi- color versions. The wall plaque was given away at trade shows along with open houses that were held at the factory sometime in the early to mid 1950s.

Wall plaque, *Rocky Mountains. Emigrants Crossing the Plains* scene, 5.4" tall, 6.75" long, Blue, **$350.00**

Markings on back

Wall plaque, *Rocky Mountains. Emigrants Crossing the Plains* scene, 5.4" tall, 6.75" long, Multicolor, **$350.00**

Markings on back

OTHER CURRIER AND IVES DINNERWARE

During research, we found that there were several other dinnerware companies that produced their own Currier and Ives wares, though. Royal China is by far the most popular probably because of the many different shapes they made and the availability of the pattern. The pieces that most closely resemble Royal China's Currier and Ives were made by Taylor, Smith and Taylor. Also, Knowles China did a "Country Life" line. Other versions were from Crooksville, Harker Pottery, Homer Laughlin, and Scio Pottery.

Taylor, Smith and Taylor.
Left: plate, 6.75"; **$2.50**;
Right: dinner plate, 10.25"; **$5.00**;
Front: soup bowl, 7.5"; **$2.50**

Detail of back stamp of
Taylor, Smith and Taylor

Anchor Hocking. Dinner plate, 10.5" wide, house in background with horses pulling a wagon in front; marked on back with "Currier & Ives Oven and Microwave Anchor Hocking Detergent Safe Ironstone Glaze." **$4.50**

GLASSWARE GO-ALONGS

It was common for designers to move from one company to another, sometimes going from dinnerware to glassware or vice versa. When they moved, they would take their ideas with them. It was reasonable to assume that if something was selling well for the old company, there may be an opportunity to advance sales for their new company. While Currier and Ives sales were expanding for Royal China, it seems that several glass companies decided to make glassware to go along with the dinnerware pieces, and to make their own versions of Currier and Ives pieces in glass. Two of the companies made glassware that could be used in the oven. They featured milk glass with a fired on blue paint of the particular scene.

McKee Glass was founded in 1853 and was one of the largest producers of pressed crystal glassware for the table. It was located in Jeannette, Pennsylvania, and continued to operate until 1951, when McKee Glass was sold to Thatcher Glass.

McKee tried to develop their own line of bake ware to compete with Corning's Pyrex, which had been introduced in 1915. The consumer loved glassware that could be used in the oven and sales of Pyrex were brisk. In 1917, McKee introduced their bake ware line, which they called Glasbake. The glass was made in both crystal and milk glass. While looking at what the consumer was buying, McKee decided to make some items to coordinate with the various Currier and Ives dinnerware. The distinctive blue scenes set against a milk glass background sold well. Various shapes were made. The bakeware is marked on the bottom with "Glasbake."

Covered baker, round, *Home to Thanksgiving* scene, 8.5" x 10"; Glasbake. **$24.50**

Covered baker, 1-quart oval, *Midnight Race on the Mississippi* scene, 4.25" tall, 6" wide, 10" long; marked on the bottom: "Made in USA Glasbake J–235 1 QT. 2." **$22.50**

Baker, square, *Harvest* scene, 2.25" tall, 8.5" wide, 8.5" long; Glasbake. **$14.50**

Baker, square, *Woodcock Shooting* scene, 2.25" tall, 8.5" wide, 8.5" long; Glasbake. **$14.50**

Bowl, oval, *The Road, –Winter* scene, 2-part, Milk Glass, 8.5" wide, 11.8" long; McKee Glasbake. **$14.50**

Loaf pan, *Harvest* scene, Milk Glass, 2.75" tall, 5" wide, 10" long;
McKee Glasbake. **$12.50**

Bowl, "Fisherman's Cottage" scene, stick handle,
Milk Glass, 1.8" tall, 5" wide without handle; Glasbake. **$12.50**

Hocking Glass began in 1905, was named for the nearby Hocking River in Lancaster, Ohio, and produced pressed dinnerware. In 1937, they merged with the **Anchor Glass** and the company was renamed **Anchor Hocking** to honor both companies. After the completion of this merger the company started working on a new type of glass that could be used in the oven. A line called Fire King was introduced in 1942 and this glassware continued until the late 1980s. It was felt that if they could market their glassware with dinnerware, they could increase their sales.

A decision was made to purchase the Taylor Smith Taylor Company in 1971, which already had a line of Currier and Ives dinnerware. Anchor Hocking began manufacturing bake ware items to compliment these items. The bake ware items were marked with the Anchor Hocking mark. There were eleven items in this assortment: a 1-quart covered casserole; a 1½-quart covered casserole; an 8-inch round cake pan; an 8-inch square cake pan; a 5 x 9-inch loaf pan; a 6½ x 10½-inch rectangular pan; a 6-ounce custard; a 12-ounce tab handle open casserole; a 1-quart mixing bowl; 1½-quart mixing bowl; and a2½-quart mixing bowl. Even though the Fire King bake ware was meant to go with the Currier and Ives from Taylor Smith Taylor, most Royal collectors eagerly add these pieces to go with their dinnerware.

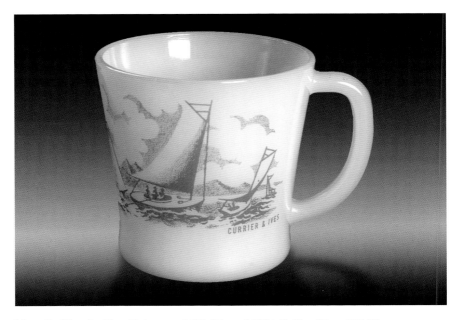

Mug, *Trolling for Blue Fish* scene, Milk Glass, 4.75" tall; Fire King, **$19.50**

Mug, *The Old Farm Gate* scene, Milk Glass, 3.4" tall; Fire King. **$17.50**

A company called **Mar-Crest** marketed some Currier and Ives ovenware through the A & P Supermarkets. We believe that Mar-Crest was a distributing company since they provided different types of items to different grocery stores. The boxes distributed to the grocery stores were marked: "A Mar-Crest Product by Marshall-Burns Division of Technicolor, Inc." We could not find any information about this company. A & P are the initials for the Great Atlantic and Pacific Tea Company, Inc. Today they are the largest grocery store chain in the northeastern United States. The Currier and Ives sales seemed to have occurred during the early to mid-1970s. A booklet was produced to announce the upcoming specialty items in a particular week. Based on the amount of your purchase, you could receive the item free or at a reduced price. When you made purchases at the market, you received coupons that were good against the cost of the featured items of the week. If you combined the coupons with the weekly sale, you could obtain the item at a nominal price.

Baker, round cake pan, Winter in the Country: *The Old Grist Mill* scene, milk glass, tab handles, 8.5" wide, 2" tall; Mar-Crest, no mark on bottom. **$16.50**

Mixing bowl,
"Fisherman's
Cottage" scene,
tab handles,
Milk Glass, 1.5
pint; Mar-Crest.
$18.50

Mixing bowl,
*The Express
Train* scene, tab
handles, Milk
Glass, 1-quart;
Mar-Crest.
$24.50

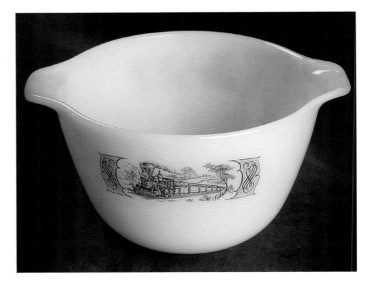

Mixing
bowl, *Early
Winter*
scene, tab
handles,
Milk Glass,
1.5-quart;
Mar-Crest.
$28.50

Mixing bowl, *Harvest* scene, tab handles, Milk Glass, 2.5-quart; Mar-Crest. **$38.50**

Custard, *Fashionable "Turn-outs" in Central Park* scene,Milk Glass, scalloped top, 2" tall, 3.75" wide; Mar-Crest, no mark. **$6.50**

Placemats, set of four, *Winter in the Country: The Old Grist Mill* scene, vinyl with foam backing; Mar-Crest. **$150**. **Note:** These are very hard to find since they were made to be used and, when they were worn, they were thrown away.

It is our feeling that there is a link between Anchor Hocking and Mar-Crest bake ware items. The shape of the items are the same, but some items are marked or and some are not. Our guess is that, when Anchor Hocking made the items as a special order for Mar-Crest, it was specified that the items have no mark on them.

Hazel Atlas was another glass company that produced Currier and Ives items, but they only seem to have made tableware. Hazel Glass was formed in 1885 and began making the milk glass liners for the zinc lids of fruit jars. Atlas Glass was founded in 1886 and first made fruit jars. The two companies merged in 1902. They later were a significant producer of tableware. They introduced a type of milk glass in the 1940s that was called "Platonite." It is assumed that while the popular blue and white Currier and Ives dinnerware was selling well, Hazel Atlas decided to make some tumblers to go with them. The dark blue scenes set against the white background were very striking. The tumblers are marked on the bottom with a stylized H set above a capital A.

Mug, *The Trout Stream* scene, Platonite, 3.4" tall; Hazel Atlas. **$12.50**

Top left: Tumbler, "Summertime" with horse-drawn carriage, one of three scenes, Platonite with dark blue paint, 5" tall, 2.75" wide, 10 ounces; Hazel Atlas Glass Company, marked HA on bottom. **$12.50**

Top right: Tumbler, "Steam Traveler" with a sternwheeler, one of three scenes, Platonite with dark blue paint, 5" tall, 2.75" wide, 10 ounces; Hazel Atlas Glass Company, marked HA on bottom. **$12.50**

Left: Tumbler, "Currier & Ives" with locomotive, one of three scenes, Platonite with dark blue paint, 5" tall, 2.75" wide, 10 ounces; Hazel Atlas Glass Company, marked HA on bottom. **$12.50**

The **Gay Fad Studio** was, as the name suggests, only a decorating company that was located in Lancaster, Ohio, and operated from 1950 to 1963. They purchased plain crystal glass from different companies to make water sets. The tapered tumblers with a plain bottom were from Libbey Glass. The shape is similar to what Libbey was making for the "Golden Foliage" line. The pitcher and tumblers were then decorated with Gay Fad Studio's own specifications and marketed under their label. The glass was left transparent or given a satin finish. The design was applied to the glass by using a silk screen process. These tumblers are frequently referred to as painted tumblers. Hazel Marie Weatherman wrote a wonderful book on this subject, called *The Painted Tumblers*.

Tumblers, crystal satin with dark blue design, 3.75" tall; Gay Fad Studio. **$9.50 each. Left to Right:** *The Road, –Winter, Early Winter, The Express Train,* and *On the Mississippi: Loading Cotton*

Detail of *The Road, –Winter* scene tumbler

Detail of *Early Winter* scene tumbler

Detail of *The Express Train* scene tumbler

Detail of *On the Mississippi: Loading Cotton* scene tumbler

Tumbler, *Winter in the Country: Getting Ice* scene, crystal satin, 5.1" tall; Gay Fad Studio. **$9.50**

Tumbler, *Winter in the Country: The Old Grist Mill*, crystal with blue and white matte silk screen, 5.5" tall; Libbey Glass. **$12.50**

Tumblers, crystal with dark blue and white silk screen, Libbey Glass.
Left: juice, *Low Water in the Mississippi* scene, 3.5" tall, 6 ounces. **$7.50**.
Right: high-ball, *Star of the Road* scene, 3.25" tall, 7 ounces. **$8.50**

Tumblers, crystal with dark blue and white silk screen; Libbey Glass
Left: juice, *Low Water in the Mississippi* scene, 3" tall, 3.5 oz; **$9.50.**
Center left: high-ball, F*ashionable "Turn-outs"*
in Central Park scene, 3.25" tall, 5 oz. **$9.50**.
Center right: water, *The Old Farm Gate* scene, 4.75" tall, 8 oz. **$12.50**.
Right: iced tea, *Winter in the Country:*
The Old Grist Mill scene, 5.6" tall, 12 oz. **$12.50**

COLLECTOR INFORMATION

No matter what pattern or color you collect, we encourage you to belong to an organization that works to preserve the history of the American pottery-making industry.

All of the resources listed below provide information by publishing an educational newsletter, doing study guides, reprinting company catalogs, doing seminars, holding a convention, having a museum and/or presenting other educational activities.

Currier and Ives Collectors Club

www.currierandivesdinnerware.com

This Currier and Ives Collectors Club was established in August 1996 to provide a place to obtain accurate information about the Currier and Ives Dinnerware or any other Royal China pattern. Its purpose was provide a forum for people who shared their love for this dinnerware and a place where they could meet. A newsletter was set up for an exchange of information.

As membership increased, an annual membership directory was established. An annual convention is also held in mid-July. (The 2015 convention for the club's 20-year Anniversary will be meeting in Royal China's hometown—Sebring, Ohio)

Membership is $15 per year for an individual, which includes four issues of the quarterly newsletter. Their website has more detailed, up-to-date information about the club and its meetings, and how to become a member.

Sebring Historical Society

www.sebringohiohistoricalsociety.org/currierives.html

The Sebring Historical Society was formed in 1988 to preserve the local heritage and history of the various pottery companies that operated in the area. The co-founders were Daphne Cannell and Dery Zeppernick, but there were many other individuals who also assisted with its formation. The following year the charter and by-laws were written allowing for the preservation and gathering of local information.

The historic Strand Theater was donated to the society in 1990 to be used as museum. Restoration took place and the theater was transformed to resemble a building from the 1940s. After many donations and fundraisers, the museum is now a show place for local history and the pottery companies from Sebring. For more information, see their website

Replacements, Ltd.

Replacements, Ltd., located at 1089 Knox Road in Greensboro, North Carolina, is a great place to find many patterns. A huge staff is on hand to help you. To see if they carry your pattern, call them at 1-800-737-5223 or go on their web site at **www.replacements.com**. If they don't have it on hand, they will actively search for it and let you know when they have located it. If a pattern isn't normally handled, but they receive numerous requests for it, they will make an attempt to have it in stock.

Another valued service is their ability to identify a pattern for you. If you have some pieces and want more, but don't know the name, you can email Replacements a photo, along with any markings, and they will gladly see if they can be of help. They have a tremendous data base to do research.

BIBLIOGRAPHY

Books

Aupperle, Eldon. *A Collector's Guide to Currier & Ives Dinnerware by Royal China Co.* Monmouth, Illinois: Seybold Printing, 1996.

Coe, Debbie and Randy. *Corning Pyroceram Cookware.* Atglen, Pennsylvania: Schiffer Publishing, 2009.

Collector Books. *Garage Sale and Flea Market Annual.* Paducah, Kentucky: Collector Books, 2009.

Collector Books. *Schroeder's Antiques Price Guide.* Paducah, Kentucky: Collector Books.

Cunningham, Jo. *The Best of Collectible Dinnerware.* Atglen, Pennsylvania: Schiffer Publishing, 1995.

Cunningham, Jo. *The Collector's Encyclopedia of American Dinnerware.* Paducah, Kentucky: Collector Books, 1982.

Florence, Gene. *Fire King.* Paducah, Kentucky: Collector Books, 1982.

Florence, Gene. *Hazel Atlas.* Paducah, Kentucky: Collector Books, 1982.

Frederiksen, Dale, Bob Page, and Dean Six. *Homer Laughlin.* Greensboro, North Carolina: Page/ Frederiksen Publications, 2003.

Hopper, Philip. *Anchor Hocking Decorated Pitchers & Glasses: The Depression Years.* Atglen, Pennsylvania: Schiffer Publishing, 2002.

Hopper, Philip. *Anchor Hocking Decorated Pitchers & Glasses: The Fire King Years.* Atglen, Pennsylvania: Schiffer Publishing, 2002.

Keller, Joe and David Ross. *Fire King An Information and Price Guide.* Atglen, Pennsylvania: Schiffer Publishing, 2002.

Kilgo, Garry & Dale, and Jerry & Gail Wilkins. *A Collectors Guide to Anchor Hocking's Fire King Glassware.* Addison, Alabama: K & W Collectibles, 1991.

Kilgo, Garry & Dale, and Jerry & Gail Wilkins. *A Collectors Guide to Anchor Hocking's Fire King Glassware, Volume II.* Addison, Alabama: K & W Collectibles, 1997.

Lehner, Lois. *Complete Book of American Kitchen and Dinner Wares.* Des Moines, Iowa: Wallace- Homestead, 1980.

Peters, Harry T. *Currier and Ives Printmakers to the American Public.* Garden City, New York: Doubleday, Doran & Co., Inc, 1942.

Rinker, Harry L. *Dinnerware of the 20th Century: The Top 500 Patterns.* New York, New York: House of Collectibles, 1997.

Six, Dean. *West Virginia Glass Town.* Charlestown, West Virginia: Quarrier Press, 2012.

Stout, Sandra McPhee Stout. *The Complete Book of McKee Glass.* North Kansas City, Missouri: Trojan Press, 1972.

Weatherman, Hazel Marie. *Glassware of the Depression Era, Book II.* Springfield, Missouri: Weatherman Glassbooks, 1974.

Weatherman, Hazel Marie. *Painted Tumbler.* Springfield, Missouri: Weatherman Glassbooks, 1978.

Emails and Phone Calls

Lisa Conklin, Replacements, Ltd., Public Relations Manager

Jaime Robinson, Replacements, Ltd., Researcher

Tim Merli, President of Currier and Ives Collector's Club

Web Sites

A & P Supermarkets: www.aptea.com/our-company

Currier and Ives Collectors Club: www.currierandivesdinnerware.com

Currier and Ives Prints: www.currierandives.com; http://freepages.rootsweb.ancestry.com/~vstern/.

eBay: www.ebay.com

Replacements, Ltd.: www.replacements.com

Sebring Ohio Historical Society: www.sebringohiohistoricalsociety.org/currierives.html

Web Spawner Royal China: www.webspawner.com/users/royalchina

INDEX

Anchor Hocking, 92, 96, 100
Ashtray, 26, 40
Birth-place of Washington, The, 8, 49, 50, 64
Bowls,
    Cereal, 29, 30, 41
    Fruit, 27, 28, 87
    Soup, 31, 32, 91
    Vegetable, 33, 34, 37
Briggs, John, 19
Butter, 35, 36, 38, 46
Butterworth, James, 7
Cake plates, 20, 31, 71-75
Calendar plate, 70
Cameron, John, 7
Candy Dish, 20, 37
Casserole, 38-40
Central Park, the Drive, 9, 26, 38-40
Clipper Ship Dreadnought–Off Tuskar Light, 9, 85, 86
Clock, 41
Coca Cola, 20
Creamer, 42, 43
Cup and Saucer, 19, 44
Currier, Charles, 6
Currier, Nathaniel, 6, 7
Denning, Charles, 41
Deviled egg dish, 20, 45
Dip Bowl, 20, 31
Durrie; George, 7, 8, 18
Early Winter, 9, 22, 31, 32, 56, 57, 67, 69, 98, 102, 103
Express Train, The, 10, 42, 43, 54, 98, 102, 103
Fashionable "Turn-outs" in Central Park, 10, 22, 35, 36, 38- 40,
    54, 55, 79, 80, 99, 105
Fire King, 96, 97, 99
"Fisherman's Cottage," 98
French Saxon Company, 20

Gay Fad Decorating, 102
Getting Ice, see *Winter in the Country: Getting Ice*
Glasbake, 93-95
Gravy boat, 46-50
Gravy ladle, 46, 50, 51
Harvest, 10, 63, 87, 94, 95, 99
Hazel Atlas Glass, 100, 101
Hebenstreit, William, 19
Home on the Mississippi, A, 11, 56, 60
Home, Sweet Home, 11, 34
Home to Thanksgiving, 11, 56, 71, 72, 93
"Homestead," see *Home to Thanksgiving*
Hostette server, 52
Hurricane lamp, 53
Ives, James, 6, 7
Jeannette Glass, 20, 25, 61
Johnson, Eastman, 7
Knirsch, Otto, 7
Libbey Glass, 102, 104, 105
Low Water in the Mississippi, 12, 44, 45, 104, 105
Maple Sugaring: Early Spring in the Northern Woods, 12, 23, 33, 37, 56
Mar-Crest, 97-100
McKee Glass, 92, 93
Midnight Race on the Mississippi, 12, 93
Milk Glass, 92-95, 97-100
Miller, Beatrice, 19
Miss Mary's Velvet Cake, 71, 73, 74
Mug, 54, 55, 96, 97, 100
Old Farm Gate, The, 13, 27, 28, 87, 97, 105
Old Grist Mill, see *Winter in the Country: The Old Grist Mill*
"Old Inn—Winter," 8, 18, 56, 78
Old Oaken Bucket, The, 13, 46, 47, 50
On the Mississippi: Loading Cotton, 13, 81-84, 102, 103
On the Road to Boston, 8, 18
Parsons, Charles, 7
Pastry server, 55
Pie baker, 20, 56- 62
Place mats, 99

Plates
    Chop, 52, 76, 77
    Dessert, 20, 63, 67- 69
    Dinner, 19, 52, 91
    Lunch, 66
    Salad, 64
    Snack, 65
Platter, 78
Preparing for Market, 14, 72
Red School House, The, 8, 18
Return from the Pasture, The, 14, 56, 59
Road, –Winter, The, 14, 35, 36, 46, 48, 50, 59, 61, 62, 94, 102, 103
Rocky Mountains—Emigrants Crossing the Plains, 15, 23, 76, 88- 90
"Schoolhouse in Winter, The," 8, 18, 29, 41
Shakers, 79, 80, 86
Sleigh Race, The, 15, 73
Snowy Morning, A, 15, 52, 56, 58, 76, 77, 89
Star of the Road, The, 16, 44, 104
"Steam Traveler," 101
Suburban Retreat, 16, 29, 30
Sugar bowl, 81-84
"Summertime," 101
Tait, Arthur Fitzwilliam, 7
Taylor, Smith, Taylor, 91, 96
Teapot, 85
Three-tier server, 87
Tile trivet, 88
Tray, 89
Trolling for Blue Fish, 16, 96
Trout Stream, 17, 100
Tumblers, 101- 105,
Venino; Franz, 7
Walker, William, 7
Wall plaque, 90
Winter in the Country: Getting Ice, 8, 17, 18, 56, 59-61, 71, 75- 77,
    104
Winter in the Country: The Old Grist Mill, 8, 17, 18, 23, 45, 53, 56,
    65- 69, 87, 97, 99, 104, 105
Woodcock Shooting, 18, 84
Worth, Thomas, 7